Deliver Us
from
The Evil One

Robert G. Bayley

Presbyterian Renewal Publications

Scripture taken from the Holy Bible, New International Version. Copyrighted© 1978 by the New York International Bible Society. Used by permission of Zondervan Bible Publishers.

First Printing 1989

DELIVER US FROM THE EVIL ONE
Copyright© 1989 by Presbyterian Renewal Publications, a subsidiary of Presbyterian and Reformed Renewal Ministries International, Inc., 2245 N.W. 39th Street, Oklahoma City, OK 73112-8886.
ISBN 0-934421-09-9

All rights reserved.
Printed in the United States of America.

Contents

Introduction 5
I. Deliverance: A Personal Testimony 9
II. Deliverance: What Is It? 12
    The Evil One 12
    The Demonic 13
    Jesus and The Demonic 15
    The Ministry of the Disciples and Apostles 16
III. Deliverance: Why Is It Needed? 17
    Sin and Disobedience 17
    The Occult 18
    Cultural Influences 19
IV. Deliverance: For Whom Is This Ministry Intended? 22
    Can a Christian Have a Demon? 23
    What About the Demonically-Afflicted Non-Christian? 24
V. Deliverance: What is Involved? 27
    Deliverance Sessions 27
    The Ministry Team 28
    Authority 30
    Discernment 30
VI. Deliverance: A Twelve-Step Process 33
VII. Deliverance: How Can It Be Kept In Perspective? 41
Endnotes 43
Appendices 44
Bibliography 47

Art thou not God the Liberator? One alone is able to liberate us in a decisive manner. It is thou. We know now that thou art the great liberator. Thou hast personally opposed thyself to the Evil One, to this usurper whose sway must be abolished because it has nothing to do with thy creation. Thou hast stepped forward to break the powers of this realm of the Devil. Thou hast caused the Devil to fall like lightening from the sky; we have seen him fall...

We no longer have to let ourselves be affected by the threat of the Evil One, nor do we need to fear it. And this is why we pray: "Lead us not into temptation, but deliver us from the Evil One." Be present in our midst, thou faithful and infallible guide, thou who showest us thy way and openest it before our feet.[1]

Karl Barth, *Prayer*

Introduction

In its excellent report entitled "The Work of the Holy Spirit," the General Assembly of the United Presbyterian Church made the following observations on exorcism:

> The Gospels tell us about "unclean spirits;" the disciples are sent forth to "cast out demons," among other commissions given to them. John's Gospel tells us that the devil is the Father of Lies,' and that he entered into Judas.
>
> How are we to interpret these evidences in the life of Jesus of his recognition of demonic spirits? Shall we dismiss the problem by saying it is only a question of terminology? Or, shall we allegorize the occasions of demonic possession? Or, shall we conclude that the accounts represent a cultural limitation, reflecting the limited knowledge of the period? Or, shall we say flatly that what the New Testament calls demon possession we would probably call neuroses or psychotic states of being? And in the wilderness, shall we say that the adversary whom Jesus met in the story is a personification of evil?
>
> Each of these conclusions is possible, and each represents a facet of the many-sided problem of demon possession; but what no amount of demythologizing can do is to discount the possibility that Jesus saw a dark reality which we often miss in our devotion to rationality, important as reason clearly is for any mature understanding of the Christian faith.
>
> Is it not conceivable that beyond the testing of his nature and the uses of his powers, Jesus saw something more? Can we not assume that beneath the outward appearance of illness and psychoses, Jesus sometimes perceived a malignant force at work whose purpose was ever to bring sickness where there was health, division where there was wholeness, and death where there was life? Does it not seem likely that the one in whom truth and life were united in an unprecedented singleness of will

should be extraordinarily perceptive about that which is the enemy of truth and life? Might it not be true that Jesus saw illness as clearly and accurately as we see it, both emotional and physical, but that he saw something else in some instances, a shadow behind the divisiveness, an adversary, an anti-Christ?[2]

Against this backdrop we hear these words, "When you pray, say ... 'deliver us from evil.'" Of all the petitions in the Lord's prayer, this undoubtedly remains the least understood. Found only in Matthew 6:13 (Luke 11:4 omits the phrase), the Greek contains the definite article, making possible legitimate alternate readings: "save us from the evil one,"[3] "deliver us from the evil one,"[4] and "keep us safe from the Evil One,"[5].

Translations that render evil a concept, "deliver us from evil," rather than a personality, "deliver us from the evil one," diminish the prayer's intensity. Evil as a concept we can live with. Evil as a personality, however, is troublesome; it forces us to reckon with a reality we prefer not to recognize.

The Confession of 1967 of the Presbyterian Church (U.S.A.) describes the reconciling act of God in Jesus Christ as, among other things, a "victory over the powers of evil."[6] To what extent was this victory accomplished on the cross? To what extent are we to be engaged in enforcing that victory? These are questions the sixth petition of The Lord's Prayer raises.

If we take seriously Christ's work on the cross, we must also stand with God against evil, not only against evil in general, but against that evil one of whom Jesus spoke as He faced Calvary as recorded in John 12:31: "Now is the time for judgement on this world; now the prince of this world will be driven out."

Paul testified before King Agrippa in Acts 26:18 that this risen Jesus had called him to minister to the Gentiles, "...to open their eyes and turn them from darkness to light, and from the power of Satan to God..." This transfer of ownership and allegiance can be instantaneous, but where the power of Satan is an explicit part of a person's life, a process is often involved. This process is commonly referred to as deliverance.

Whatever a person's theology, the reality of evil in sometimes frightening, demonic forms require the follower of Jesus Christ to seek an effective response. As we reflect on the encounters between Jesus and those tormented by the powers of darkness, and similar encounters in the early church, we can discover timeless principles still viable for Christians today.

A word of caution: the twin dangers of denying the evil one's existence and attributing all brokenness to him are ever before us. In seeking to identify the source of evil in any given situation, our own hearts' potential for every conceivable evil must always be seriously considered. Only as we distinguish the demonic from the human can we deal effectively with either.

DISCUSSION QUESTIONS:
1. Up until now, how have you understood the sixth petition of The Lord's Prayer, "deliver us from evil"?
2. Have you ever sensed the presence of evil in some way that exceeded your ability to understand or deal with it? Reflect on those times and relate them to the prayer "deliver us from evil."
3. Is the concept of demons as real entities troublesome to you? If so, consider your concerns in light of the gospel accounts of Jesus' encounters with demons. What conclusions do you draw?

I
Deliverance: A Personal Testimony

The spiritist medium looked into my eyes and into those of my twin baby brother. About my brother she said nothing. But of me she said: "He's an old soul. He's been here many times before." It would prove a troublesome and tormenting observation.

As I was growing up, our family visited this woman — whom we called an aunt — many times. Through personal conversation, books, periodicals and letters, this "aunt" cultivated in me an interest in the occult. When I was twelve or so, she led me into her back yard to the crotch of a tree where, she explained, an angelic spirit appeared and instructed her. There she instructed me in occult ways.

This exposure stimulated an intense religious search that led me through traditional cults and into bizarre spiritist and occult groups, each influencing me as I passed through. I remained active during this entire time in our local Presbyterian church — singing in the choir, serving as president of the youth group and teaching Sunday school.

Then when I was seventeen, at a meeting at my grandmother's church I heard the simple message of a personal relationship with Jesus Christ and turned my life over to the One I had been misinterpreting through cult and occult teachings. From that moment on, I was freed of all the false teachings I had embraced.

While I left all my occult beliefs behind at my conversion, I did not leave behind all the spiritual effects of my occult practices. I began to notice this after entering a Christian college where spiritual gifts were exercised. I began to manifest certain gifts which I was assured were from the Lord. As I yielded to these "gifts," I received continued affirmation from other Christians. What they didn't know was that along with these "gifts" came a sense of encircling darkness that I felt was threatening my life. God's gifts should bring peace and light, I reasoned, but these spiritual abilities were bringing darkness, confusion and fear.

I began to pray earnestly about this. Before long an area pastor came into my life who believed in something I had never heard of before: deliverance.

As I described to him what was happening to me, he recognized the presence of demonic spirits, and I recognized that whatever was giving me these powers was not from God. I also became aware that along with my desire to be freed from this tormenting spiritual power a part of me was fascinated with it, drawn to it. I wanted to be free of it, yet was reluctant to give it up. The spiritual power given by the evil one, I learned, has its own perverted attraction.

In a series of prayer sessions with this pastor, I confessed the Lordship of Jesus and repented of sin in my life. Finally, when we were ready to address the demonic spirits themselves, this man of God spoke to them with quiet authority: "In the name of Jesus, I command you to name yourselves."

At this command a voice not my own responded: "We are of the spirits of the magicians that duplicated the works of Moses before Pharaoh." (See Exodus 7:6-12.)

With the authority of Christ the pastor continued, "I command you now to come out in the name of Jesus, to never torment Bob again, and to go to the pit of hell to never torment anyone again." At once, without another word, they left.

I immediately felt free, light, clean and whole. The ancient spirits that had given me "an old soul" from birth, that had imparted supernatural power to imitate spiritual gifts from God, had left me.

I spent the next five years, however, unwilling and unable to allow the Holy Spirit to evidence any of His gifts in my life, so afraid was I of the false. The absence of sensitive follow-up ministry extended this time unnecessarily.

Today I know a comfortable, confident working of the Holy

spirit in my life through spiritual gifts. As He works in and through me, in contrast to the fear and darkness of the past, I experience joy, peace and freedom.

When I pray "deliver us from evil," I know from experience at least part of what that means. I can also testify that Jesus answers the prayers He gives us to pray. He does indeed deliver us from the evil one!

DISCUSSION QUESTIONS:
1. How do you feel about this account?
2. Have you ever read about or heard someone describe his or her deliverance from demonic powers? If so, what was your reaction then? How are those accounts like or unlike the account you have just read?
3. If such things happened in the ministry of Jesus and the ministry of the early church, is it possible that such things still happen today? Why or why not?

II
Deliverance: What is It?

The biblical idea of God as deliverer originates in the deliverance of the Israelites from bondage in Egypt. This act became the predominant theme of Jewish history.

So when Jesus gave His disciples a pattern for prayer that included a petition for deliverance from the evil one, it did not sound foreign to their ears. They had grown up in a culture grounded in the delivering act of God.

They had also been privileged to observe firsthand the delivering work of Jesus in His earthly ministry. "...the people brought to Jesus all the sick and demon-possessed. The whole town gathered at the door, and Jesus healed many who had various diseases. He also drove out many demons ... He traveled throughout Galilee, preaching in their synagogues and driving out demons" (Mark 1:32-34, 39).

The Evil One

The Lord's Prayer petition for deliverance specifically names "the evil one." Who is this evil one?

While sometimes referred to as the enemy, the prince of this world or the adversary, three biblical names warrant our special attention.

SATAN — From the Hebrew "satana," Satan means adversary or wicked opponent, and appears in the New Testament as often as the word "devil."

DEVIL — From the Greek "diabalos," devil means slanderer. It can also mean to accuse, to bring charges with hostile intent, and to divide. "Diabalos" consists of the preposition "dia" meaning "through," and the verb "ballo" meaning "to throw," yielding a literal definition of "to throw through." The devil then is the one who seeks to throw something through the middle of our individual and corporate lives (as churches) to divide and confuse us.

John Calvin in his Institutes observes that "...since the devil was created by God, let us remember that this malice, which we attribute to his nature, came not from his creation but his perversion. For, whatever he has that is to be condemned he has derived from his revolt and fall."[7]

BEELZEBUB — Possibly of Aramaic or Hittite origin, this name means "Lord (baal) of the flies (zebub)." In Matthew 12:22-28, Jesus used this name to describe the prince of demons who, like flies, are viewed as unseen inhabitants of the air.

The evil one is also called the tempter (Matthew 4:3, 1 Thessalonians 3:5), a dragon (Revelation 12:3), a serpent (Revelation 12:9), the destroyer (Revelation 9:11), ruler of the kingdom of the air (Ephesians 2:2), and prince of this world (John 12:31; 14:30; 16:11).

The Demonic

The concept of the demonic, while present in the Old Testament, was not fully developed until the ministry of Jesus and the writing of the New Testament. Deuteronomy 18:10-14 clearly links occult practices with the demonic. Deuteronomy 32:17 indicates that all the gods of the surrounding peoples were demonic in origin and nature, a concept repeated by Paul in his letter to the Corinthians newly set free from idol worship (1 Corinthians 10:19-21). Finally, the psalmist understands that the neighboring peoples who sacrificed their children to idols, a practice in which unfaithful Jews also participated, actually did so to demonic powers (Psalm 106:36-37).

The idea of a person being possessed by or delivered from a demonic power is reserved for the New Testament writers to develop. They had three sources: first, their witness of encounters between Jesus and the demonic, recorded in the gospels; second, Jesus' commissioning of the writers and others to exercise authority over demonic spirits; and third, the early church's witness of power encounters between the Holy Spirit and the demonic.

Two interchangeable terms are used in the New Testament for these demonic powers: demons and spirits, sometimes called "unclean" or "evil" spirits.

DEMON — From the Greek "daimonion," the designation originally referred to minor Greek deities and, in popular belief, the spirits of the departed. In New Testament usage the term became an explicit reference to specific evil entities, traditionally the angels who fell with Satan in the rebellion against God at some point in the unwritten past (Revelation 12:7-9; 2 Peter 2:4). Jesus referred to this fall of Satan in the context of a ministry of the seventy-two whom he had sent out with authority over demons (Luke 10:17-20).

SPIRITS — From the same Greek term used for the Spirit of God, "pneuma," it is used regularly by itself to refer to the spirits of the evil one throughout the gospels and Acts.

UNCLEAN SPIRITS — Here, "pneuma" is preceded by the adjective "akatharton" — unclean. The Greek word for clean (from which we get such English words as catharsis and cathartic) is negated by the prefix "a" (as in atheist). Part of the ministry of Jesus is to make clean, through deliverance, those possessed by what is unclean, the demonic. (Mark 1:23-27; 5:1-20; 7:25-30; Acts 5:16; 8:7; Revelation 16:13).

EVIL SPIRITS — In this instance "pneuma" is joined with "poneros" rendering "evil spirits" (Acts 19:12-16). The noun form appears in the Lord's Prayer in the sixth petition, "but deliver us from 'tou ponerou,' the evil one." The designation is also assigned to Satan in the parable of the sower in Matthew 13:19, and to the larger forces against which we engage in spiritual battle as referred to in Paul's letter to the Ephesians, 6:12: "For our struggle is not against flesh and blood, but against ... the spiritual forces of evil (ta pneumatika tes ponerias)."

By whatever name they are called, it is clear that Jesus, those whom He sent out in His name, and those who embraced Him in the early church both recognized the real presence of demonic or evil spirits and knew an authority from God empowering them to deal with them. This ministry to those afflicted with such spirit entities is known as deliverance or exorcism.

The Ministry of Jesus

Three stages in the development of the ministry of deliverance are identifiable in Scripture: in the ministry of Jesus Himself, that of His immediate followers (disciples and apostles), and that of the early church. Detailed scriptural charts may be found for each stage in the appendices.

The foundation was laid for Jesus' ministry to those afflicted by demonic powers when the evil one attempted to thwart the ministry of Jesus during forty days of temptation in the wilderness. Jesus emerged unscathed and undeterred, returning to Galilee "in the power of the Spirit" (Luke 4:14).

Jesus' power over the evil one and his demons demonstrated His Messiahship and the presence of the kingdom of God (Luke 11:20). Rudolf Bultmann says that Jesus "sees God's Reign already breaking in in the fact that by the divine power that fills him he is already beginning to drive out demons."[8]

From this point on Jesus regularly and authoritatively confronted the demonic as an integral part of his ministry.

The picture that emerges from a survey of Jesus' encounters with the demonic may be summarized as follows:

1. After successfully defeating Satan in the desert, Jesus regularly encountered and defeated Satan's emissaries, the evil, unclean spirits or demons.
2. Jesus never sought the encounters. Rather, those afflicted by demons sought Him, recognizing His power to deliver them.
3. Jesus was recognized as having authority in His teaching because of His ability to control and cast out evil spirits.
4. While physical afflictions of some were attributed to demonic powers, others identically afflicted were not treated as demonized. Demonic activity might cause some illnesses, but definitely not all. Jesus could discern the difference.
5. Jesus willingly went to the cross, knowing He would there remove the evil one from his position of power in the world and enable subsequent generations to be freed from the powers of the evil one.

The Ministry of the Disciples and Apostles

Having beaten Satan at his own game, identified as death in Hebrews 2:14, Jesus gave His post-resurrection followers this ministry of deliverance. This post-resurrection power over the demonic, even over Satan himself, was not limited to Paul's ministry as is shown by the ministry of Philip (Acts 8:4-8). The concept of the relationship between the believer and the evil one, and the believer's power over the evil one and his evil spirits, continued to be developed in the early church.

Finally, the apocalyptic record of Saint John the Divine, in banishment on the Isle of Patmos, is filled with a visionary account of the struggle between light and darkness, good and evil, Jesus and Satan. In the end, the deceiving devil, the beast and false prophet of Revelation, along with death and hell, are thrown into the lake of fire by Jesus (Revelation 20:10,14). Sometimes reading the end of a book first can provide a sense of security and excitement in reading the rest of it!

Such spiritual warfare is no less needed today then it was in the early church. Twentieth-century Anglican clergyman Michael Harper writes: "The early Christians often seem to have viewed their experience in terms of warfare ... This same spiritual warfare goes on today. It will increase as the end of the age draws nearer, and Christ's return becomes imminent. The basic New Testament principles of spiritual warfare remain the same, even though Satan dresses himself up in new disguises."[9]

DISCUSSION QUESTIONS:
1. As you trace God's acts as deliverer from Egypt through the ministry of Jesus and through the experiences of the early church, what do you think this reveals about God's nature?
2. Do you believe demons were and are real entities, or did Jesus simply embrace the superstitions of his day and pass them on to His church?
3. What implications does your answer to question 2 have for your attitude towards Scripture? Your relationship to the church which bases its life on Scripture? Your relationship to evil in the world?

III
Deliverance: Why is it Needed?

A ministry of deliverance is founded on two basic premises: first, that the gospel accounts of the reality of the demonic are trustworthy, and second, that the possibility exists that individuals today can be similarly afflicted and therefore in need of deliverance.

While no list of possible sources of demonic influence can be complete, the following areas represent the more common sources. A true story illustrates each area of concern.

Sin and Disobedience

CASE STUDY: A Christian man was tormented by unclean sexual thoughts. He acknowledged a sexual relationship in college with a woman heavily involved in the occult and witchcraft. Prayer for deliverance from the effects of the sexual sin and darkness was followed by a sense of release, relief and peace.

Demonic presence due to willful sin and disobedience is the compounding of an existing condition, not the introduction of a new one. In this instance sexual sin was compounded by engaging in it with someone who had yielded herself to demonic powers in the occult.

Following his willful sin, King Saul was tormented by an evil spirit (1 Samuel 16:14). Samuel was sent to tell him of the correlation between such sin and the occult: "Rebellion is like the sin of divination" (1 Samuel 15:23).

It is unwise and unhealthy to assume that every sin results in demonic affliction. It is equally unwise and unhealty, however, to believe that immersion in willful sin does not expose a person to such a risk. In discussing anger, for example, Paul reminds the Ephesians that unresolved anger can "give the devil a foothold," and so exhorts, "Do not let the sun go down while you are still angry" (Ephesians 4:26-27).

The Occult

CASE STUDY: A middle-aged woman who for years was skilled at casting horoscopes became a Christian, yet was still able to exercise her power. It brought with it an absence of peace and joy and many restless nights. After prayer for deliverance, she testified to a deep peace and joy, and nights filled with restful sleep.

Her story illustrates the continuing influence of involvement in the occult even after becoming a Christian, something to which my own testimony also points. Paul came across such an occult spirit that gave fortune-telling powers (Acts 16:16-19). Exercising the gift of discernment given by the Holy Spirit (1 Corinthians 12:10), Paul took authority over the spirit and commanded it to leave.

The prohibition of involvement in the occult is an ancient one. In Deuteronomy 18:9-13 we find God's prohibition against divination, sorcery, the interpreting of omens, witchcraft, casting spells, consulting the dead, and serving as a medium for a spirit or spiritism. The current interest in crystals and pyramids adds these to the long-standing list that includes tarot cards, tea-leaf reading, palm reading, horoscopes, astrology, ouija boards, water witching, table lifting, psychic healing, and the numerous "new age" materials currently being promoted through such avenues as "A Course in Miracles."

Some people expose themselves to demonic influence through involvement with organized religious entities that promote occult teachings and practices. These are frequently promoted as something to which people can give themselves and still remain in their own churches. "Not a religion," they will say. Paul reminds us in 1 Timothy 4:1 that there will be teachings fabricated by demons for the purpose of deceiving. Finally, eastern meditational techniques, when not severed from their non-Christian religious context and emptied of their non-Christian content, can also expose the participant to demonic influence.

Such demonic influence can be referred to as invitational since the person so afflicted invites the influence through a willful involvement in the occult. To consent to what demonic forces invent and promote — the occult — is to consent to the demonic.

Cultural Influences

CASE STUDY: A man who had taken LSD began hearing voices telling him there were many different ways to live and it didn't matter which one he chose — many ways to God and no need of a Savior. After finding Christ he was delivered from the effects of his drug involvement.[10] This young man found that an aspect of his culture that appeared to offer meaning — illegal use of drugs — was in fact deceiving.

Another cultural influence causing concern today is the wording of some of the popular music to which teens and young adults listen. When the content clearly supports rebellion against authority, abuse of drugs, the pursuit of illicit sex, and yielding allegiance to the devil, we can safely assume that a negative cultural influence is present that can open the door to demonic influence. Much of today's music sounds the same, however, and we should take care not to throw out all the music because of a few bad lyrics. God has given us the ability to think analytically and critically. Such gifts are particularly needed when considering culture as a possible source of demonic influence.

The Israelites were prohibited from worshipping the gods of the surrounding cultures (Deuteronomy 12:1-4), and Paul warned the Corinthians to avoid those things in their culture that represented their pre-Christian ways (1 Corinthians 10:14-22). Christians are to avoid the gods of every culture, visible or invisible, even as we seek to be salt and light in our culture of which they are a part and from which they benefit.

Generational Ties

CASE STUDY: A couple in their fifties made commitments to Christ, and in the process withdrew from membership and involvement in a secret fraternal organization. They experienced a measure of peace and freedom over this decision, but lacked total peace. They next recognized the need to discard a large library of books on ritual and teaching published by the group and did so. Still one thing remained — a collection of jewelry crafted for use by the organization. The jewelry represented four or five generations of involvement with the group and was a source of lingering pride in that association. They finally discarded the jewelry, and after prayer for complete freedom from the generational hold on them reported a deep peace and great joy in their lives.

In the broadest sense we all suffer from a generational bondage that goes back to Adam. The remedy for that is not deliverance from demonic influence, but conversion to Christ. The kinds of generational ties that can result in a demonic presence or effect are more specific.

The Old Testament teaches that one generation's sins affect subsequent generations (Exodus 20:4-6; I Kings 16:25, 29-32; 22:51-53). At times, therefore, individuals confessed not only their own sins but their fathers' sins, too, asking for forgiveness and freedom from the effects of both (Nehemiah 1:6; Psalms 79:8; 106).

Some frequently encountered generational ties in which the demonic might be involved include gripping fears ("My grandmother and mother were also terrified of enclosed places/heights/water/fire/etc."); sexual obsessions ("My grandfather and father were also involved in extramarital affairs/sexual abusers of their children/etc."); addictive behavior patterns, which can involve a demonic compounding of a genetic predisposition ("I come from three generations of alcoholics/compulsive gamblers/wife beaters/etc.").

In each of these kinds of situations, it is possible that no demonic spirit is present and that all symptoms are due to other causes. On the other hand, demonic compounding of existing problems may also exist. Consultation with others (medical and psychological professionals) and discernment are both needed.

The purpose of freedom from generational bondage is quite simple — that we might be free to serve God's purposes for our individual lives in our own generation.

Pornography and Sexual Sin

CASE STUDY: A fifty-year-old man recounted being sexually molested at age 12 by an older boy, resulting in a phallic fixation that followed him into adulthood. As an adult he married, then became sexually unfaithful, first with women, then with men. Pornography became a growing part of his life until it dominated him.

After turning his life over to Christ, he sought prayers for deliverance. This resulted in a complete break with sexual sin and pornography. Gone was his ability to recognize instantly other homosexually oriented men, made possible by what he described as a "possessive spirit deep inside."

This testimony comes from a respected businessman whose public and private lives, until recently, were on different tracks. He represents the growing numbers of Christian men seeking freedom from bondage to pornography. His story illustrates the constellation of factors in which a demonic compounding of events and feelings can take place. It also serves as a reminder not to assume that all sexual sin is solely demonic in origin.

As with all the areas discussed, extramarital sexual activity and exposure to pornography do not automatically lead to a demonic presence. They do, though, provide a possible opening.

This chapter only touches on some of the more common sources of demonic influence. In all situations where the demonic might be present, discernment combined with consultation with others provides the spiritual and relational atmosphere most conducive to a ministry of deliverance, if needed, and to addressing the healing needs of the whole person.

DISCUSSION QUESTIONS:
1. What is your response to the stories told in this chapter? Do the symptoms in one or more sound like those of anyone you know?
2. In what ways can people expose themselves to demonic influence in your community? Have you ever considered a possible demonic dimension to these areas before?
3. If any part of this chapter strikes a responsive chord in your own life and you suspect you might need help in determining whether you need deliverance, share this with someone whom you trust as a Christian and friend. Seek his or her counsel, discernment and prayer.

IV
Deliverance: For Whom is this Ministry Intended?

"There is no exception to the general impression given by the Gospels that Christ healed out of mercy in the knowledge that it is God's will to deliver men from all kinds of evil."[11]

> CASE STUDY: A 12-year old girl came for help, brought by her mother who had already consulted doctors and psychiatrists. The girl would sit and scratch herself until she bled. As prayer began for her, her face contorted. She began to dig her nails into her flesh, and a voice not her own protested the praying. Upon inquiry it was learned that the mother had occult materials in the home. She was asked if she would dispose of them. She refused. When it became clear that she did not want to follow Christ but only wanted relief for her daughter, the session concluded without the desired result.

While "it is God's will to deliver men from all kinds of evil," He will not force this work of mercy on those who resist submission to Him.

This incident points to an important principle. Deliverance from the demonic is not a matter of convenience, nor simply of alleviating discomfort, pain or suffering caused by the presence of evil spirits. It is intended, as is all of God's work on earth, to bring us to Himself.

Jesus told of an evil spirit that had gone out of a man, seeking but not finding a new place to live. The man it had left was cleansed, but empty. So the spirit returned with seven other spirits more wicked than itself, and they went in and lived there. The final condition of that man was worse than the first.

"No amount of deliverance," Michael Scanlon writes, "can

replace the central need in a person's life to accept the lordship of Jesus and to live out the reality of that commitment in concrete terms."[12]

Demons cast out in the absence of a willingness to follow and obey Christ leaves the person or "house" clean but empty, and susceptible to even worse demonic influence. Deliverance is most apt to take place and have lasting results when it involves either a non-Christian who sincerely wants to turn to Christ, or a Christian who intends to obey Christ in every area.

Can a Christian Have a Demon?

The phrase in the Gospels that is most often translated "demon-possessed" in English is "daimonion echein" (to have a demon).[13]

A person is susceptible to demonic influence, certainly before conversion when the person is without protection, and after conversion in certain circumstances. The presence of demonic influence or bondage before or after conversion may be due to one or more of the following causes: generational ties, willful serious sin or involvement in the occult.

As one reflects upon the phenomenon of being delivered from a demon or evil spirit, one concludes that a demon actually can infest or occupy the body of a Christian and perhaps even the soul or mind but not the spirit where the Holy Spirit indwells. This would suggest a trichotomous nature of humankind (see I Thessalonians 5:23-24) rather than the traditional biblically interpreted dichotomous nature. However construed, numerous Christians have been relieved of demonic influence or bondage from such a trichotomous understanding.

John Wimber tells of the deliverance of a Christian referred to him by a clinical psychologist.

CASE STUDY: "At our first meeting a demon manifested itself through Bill, which was the first time something like this had happened to him. Bill's voice and personality changed, his face became contorted, and the spirit challenged my authority to be there. Until this time Bill had ruled out the possibility that he might be under the influence of demons, because he had been taught and believed that demons could not influence Christians today.

"I said, 'Identify yourself.' They said they made Bill use pornography and practice masterbation; they caused his rage and self-hatred. I said, 'In the name of Jesus, leave Bill right now' (see Luke 10:17). At first the demons resisted my commands, so I prayed further and again told them to leave. After about thirty minutes of prayer, they were gone. Bill told me that for the first time in years he felt free from compulsions to sin sexually.

"A week later we again met with Bill, because though he no longer struggled with the desire to view pornography and make obscene phone calls, he still felt a great deal of anxiety. During this second session we cast out spirits that created fear, self-abuse, and a false religiosity.

"Recently I met with Bill, and after almost two years he is still no longer involved with pornography or obscene phone calls. He is still meeting with his psychologist, but his problems are no longer demonic."[14]

What About the Demonically-afflicted Non-Christian?

When dealing with demon-afflicted people not committed to following Christ, we need to remember Jesus' illustration of the man who, once cleansed of an evil spirit, remained empty, and ended up with more demons than before. Even if fully delivered, unless a non-Christian turns to Christ, there remains no protection from subsequent demonic attack and bondage.

Consider the following account from the history of Christian missions in the last century.

CASE STUDY: "*A native assistant of the English Wesleyan Mission, was passing along one of the streets of his native village, when he saw a small company making sport of a man who, they said, was possessed of a devil. They called to the native assistant and challenged him to come and cast out the demon, as he had claimed that the God of the Christians had such power. He went and prayed with the man, who then became much more quiet. The assistant visited him for two or three days, when he appeared to be perfectly well, and seemed to form an exceedingly strong attachment for the native assistant who had prayed for him. The circumstance led to the formation of a class which met every evening for the study of the Bible, and some were converted.*"[15]

A few years ago William Wilson, M.D., a psychiatrist on the staff of Duke University Medical Center, dealt with a case of demonization. Here is his account.

CASE STUDY: "This thirty-two-year-old, twice-married female was brought in because of falling spells which had been treated with all kinds of anticonvulsant medication. She was examined on the neurosurgical service and after all examinations including EEG, brain scan, and a pseumoencephalogram were negative, she was transferred to the psychiatric service. Her mental status examination was unremarkable and all of the staff commented that she seemed normal until she had her first 'spell.'

"While standing at the door of the day room she was violently thrown to the floor, bruising her arm severely. She was picked up and carried to her room all the while resisting violently. When I arrived, eight persons were restraining her as she thrashed about on the bed. Her facial expression was one of anger and hate. Sedation resulted in sleep.

"During the ensuing weeks, the patient was treated psychotherapeutically and it was learned that there was considerable turmoil in her childhood home, but because she was 'pretty' she was spoiled. She married the type of individual described by Jackson Smith as the first husband of an hysterical female. She was a 'high liver' and after her separation and divorce, she was threatened with rejection by her parents. She remarried and her second husband was a 'nice' but unexciting man. She continued to associate with her 'high living' friends. When her husband demanded that she give up her friends and her parties, she started having the 'spells.'

"The usual psychotherapeutic treatment for hysteria including interviews under sodium amytol only aggravated her spells. Seclusion in the closed section brought her assaultive and combative behavior to an end, but she would have spells in which she became mute, especially when religious matters were discussed. More dramatically, when the names Jesus or Christ were mentioned she would immediately go into a trance. On one occasion while in a coma, in desperation, a demon was exorcised and her spells ceased. She subsequently accepted Christ as her Savior and has been well since."[16]

The pressing question does not seem to be whether demons exist today, or even whether a Christian can be troubled by a demon. Rather the crucial question before us is: what can

Christians do to bring release into the lives of those tormented by demonic powers? The next chapter addresses this issue.

DISCUSSION QUESTIONS:
1. What is your reaction to the case studies presented? What do they say about who you are, where you live, and the people around you?
2. After reading this chapter, do you think of any situations in which a demon may have been active, but you didn't recognize it at the time? What happened in that incident?
3. Are you aware of any present situations where you suspect there may be a demonic presence influencing you or someone you know? What are the symptoms? How do you plan to handle it? What counsel do the others in your discussion group offer?

V
Deliverance: What is Involved?

We turn now to some of the specific elements that go into the deliverance ministry.

Deliverance Sessions

CASE STUDY: An elderly gentleman presented himself for prayer in a formal healing service. Upon being anointed with oil, an encircling demonic darkness became apparent. Prayer for deliverance from the bondage of many years brought tears and a smile. Ten years have passed and the man continues to report freedom from the darkness that had held him all his life.

In the Presbyterian church where this occurred, the Session wisely chose to call the monthly afternoon service a prayer service. People were invited to seek prayer for themselves or others. In that context the demonic was frequently confronted in such a way that others present remained unaware of what was taking place. In no instance did anyone indicate a demonic problem on the prayer card. In every instance the awareness came through discernment supplied by the Holy Spirit.

It is doubtful that many would come to a service called a "Deliverance Service." Experience suggests that the use of a less loaded term such as "Prayer Service" frees all involved to be open to the direction of the Holy Spirit to pray for healing, deliverance and other personal needs.

Deliverance is one facet of the healing prayer ministry. For Jesus, casting or driving out demons was part of His healing ministry, not separate from it. "People brought to him all who were ill with various diseases, those suffering severe pain, the demon-possessed, the epileptics and the paralytics, and he healed them ... At that time Jesus cured many who had diseases, sicknesses and evil spirits" (Matthew 4:24 and Luke 7:21). Those needing deliverance are viewed as being afflicted and in need of healing.

James 5:14 says, "Is any one of you sick? He should call the elders of the church to pray over him and anoint him with oil in the name of the Lord." This biblical command acknowledges two fundamental principles operative in all Christian ministry.

First, people needing help must confess their need and ask for help, something Jesus frequently asked for before healing people. It is usually better not to offer prayers of healing for the sick unless they request or consent to it. It is doubly important to observe this principle when dealing with the demonic.

Second, the context of prayers for healing and deliverance is important. When a person calls on church leaders for prayer, the ministry takes place in the context of a relationship characterized by both accountability and responsibility. This may be done in a scheduled prayer service or by private appointment with a prayer team.

Establishing a time and place for prayer ministry that is either specifically for deliverance or where there are strong indications this will be called for involves thoughtful planning. Such prayer is best conducted apart from the worship and teaching sessions of the church in a place where interruptions, distractions and the curious gazes of others can be avoided. The quiet office of a church pastor, a family room in a private home, or a Sunday school room unused during the week seem to work well.

In such prayer sessions, "the all-important fact that can never be lost is that the wounded and broken people are to be made whole. We work with persons before we work with spirits and demons; the human reality always overrides the demonic reality."[17]

The Ministry Team

Who should be involved in praying for those needing deliverance?

CASE STUDY: An elderly woman was brought for prayer for freedom from her senility. The prayer group that gathered was made up of the curious and the committed. After praying for some time, there was no change in the woman's disoriented responses. While one man prayed silently for the confused and curious in the room whose presence was interfering with the prayers for deliverance, a woman addressed the subject in a Swiss-German dialect. She immediately responded in the same dialect although she had never learned it, but in a voice not her own. Her response indicated an inability to respond in prayer. Finally the session concluded with no change.

This incident points up the seriousness of this ministry. While Jesus ministered deliverance in public surrounded by all sorts of people, we are not Jesus. We seek to be used by Him to minister His wholeness from lives that are broken — our own — to lives that are broken — others'. It would be unwise to give a hard and fast answer to the question, "Who should be present?" However, some guidelines are helpful.

"The person in charge of the session should be the one who has some overall pastoral authority over the person present for the ministry. If there is a person with more immediate pastoral authority such as parents for children, husband for his wife, or a local pastoral head or assistant pastor, this person should also be present. Normally the person in charge of the session will endeavor to have someone else present to assist him. This person should have recognized pastoral authority and experience in the deliverance ministry. Finally, if the person present for ministry is a woman, then another woman who would be most helpful both in the session and the follow-up, taking both into consideration, should be present."[18]

While the ideal model is a pastoral one, not all persons needing this ministry have pastors able to exercise it or who even believe in it. However, a reasonable attempt to receive ministry from one's own pastor should be made, asking for pastoral prayers for wholeness, freedom and peace. This very approach from humble persons seeking help has introduced some pastors to this ministry. God in His wisdom may desire to use a person's need for deliverance as a catalyst for growth of both parishioner and pastor.

Regardless of the response to the request, respect must be maintained for one's own pastor as the spiritual authority to which the person has submitted himself/herself as a member of a local church. To fail to do this could mean removing oneself from under spiritual authority, and being under authority is an essential aspect of the deliverance ministry.

Authority

CASE STUDY:
"I command you to loose your hold on Jeff in Jesus' name."
"You have no authority over me."
"I know I don't. That's why I didn't come against you in my name but in the name of Jesus who does have authority over you, and it's in His name that I command you to leave, never to torment Jeff again."
The young man being prayed for had been arrested for indecent exposure. As a Christian he desired freedom from a tormenting desire to engage in such activity. This conversation formed part of the prayer time that resulted in peace and freedom from the behavior.

Jesus illustrated this principle in His encounter with the Roman centurion (Matthew 8:5-13 and Luke 7:1-10). When Jesus offered to come and heal the centurion's sick servant, the centurion replied that it was not necessary. Jesus had only to "say the word and my servant will be healed. For I am a man under authority, with soldiers under me; and I say to one, 'Go,' and he goes, and to another, 'Come,' and he comes."

The centurion had authority over others only as long as he himself stayed under an authority his soldiers recognized. Had he removed himself from under the authority of his superiors and ultimately of Rome, he would immediately have lost all authority over his soldiers. There can be no substitute for submitting our lives to the authority of Jesus in every area. To the extent that we submit to His authority, we have it to exercise. This is a basic principle in the ministry of deliverance: authority comes from being under authority.

Discernment

CASE STUDY: *"Once when we were going to the place of prayer, we were met by a slave girl who had a spirit by which she predicted the future. She earned a great deal of money for her owners by fortune-telling. This girl followed Paul and the rest of* us shouting, 'These men are servants of the Most High God, who are telling you the way to be saved.' She kept this up for many days. Finally Paul became so troubled that he turned around and said to the spirit, 'In the name of Jesus Christ I command you to come out of her!' At that moment the spirit left her" (Acts 16:16-18).

This encounter illustrates the use of the gift of the Spirit mentioned in I Corinthians 12:10: "the ability to distinguish between spirits." Crucial to understanding this encounter between Paul and the slave girl is the recognition that what she was saying was totally true, but its source was not. Only the gift of discernment, the "ability to distinguish between spirits," enabled Paul to sense in his spirit — where "he became so troubled" — that this was not of God, and to take appropriate action in the authoritative name of Jesus under whose authority Paul had placed himself.

Michael Scanlon and Randall Cirner, both involved in the ministry of deliverance in the Roman Catholic renewal movement, write:

"Discernment is perhaps the most crucial element in deliverance. It is fundamentally a spiritual gift and as such cannot be learned or taught. The operation of the Spirit through discernment keeps the deliverance session on track and provides the inspiration and insight necessary to know how to proceed. Discernment is the main guiding force in: (1) knowing what is actually the work of an evil spirit; (2) deciding what area to deal with next; (3) knowing whether the evil spirit is truly gone; (4) revealing the presence or activity of evil spirits not already known at the time the deliverance began; (5) determining at what pace the session should proceed and how long it should last; and (6) what other forms of ministry the person may need (inner healing, counsel, repentance, strengthening, and comfort)."[19]

Deliverance sessions as part of the larger prayer ministry of the church for healing, the importance of the spiritual condition of those in a ministry team, and spiritual authority and discernment, are all important to the ministry of freedom from demonic affliction.

DISCUSSION QUESTIONS:
1. Have you ever been present where prayer for deliverance from an evil spirit was offered for someone? What happened and what did you learn?
2. Have you ever prayed for someone else and sensed something evil which you perhaps weren't able to define but which you recognized was something other than the person's sinful nature? What did you do? How did you pray?
3. Have you experienced a clear awareness of the presence of evil (the demonic) in someone else or in a situation? If so, how did you respond to this gift of discernment?
4. How important do you think the gift of discernment is in today's world and church? Give some examples of how you think this gift might prove useful.

VI
Deliverance: A Twelve-step Process

God in His wisdom did not place a sample deliverance session in the Bible, nor did He give an outline to follow. Individual situations and cases will call for individual approaches. However, there are a number of elements which will, in some way or another, usually find their way into the deliverance/healing process. While all are Scripture-based, the *sequence* is not.

These twelve steps are: recognition, request, responsibility, repentance, renunciation, rebuking, releasing, renewal, referral, restoration, relationships and redirection.

Step 1 - Recognition

"My daughter is suffering terribly from demon possession " (Matthew 15:22).

"...Jesus healed many who had various diseases. He also drove out many demons, but he would not let the demons speak ..." (Mark 1:34).

In both of these cases the starting point for deliverance is the recognition of the presence of an evil spirit. In the first instance the woman recognized this about her family member. In the second instance Jesus recognized this in those coming to be healed.

Principle: Sometimes people know themselves to be demonically influenced or bound. In other instances, part of the influence is blindness to the presence, and the discernment of others is necessary for recognition of the demonic to occur.

Step 2 - Request

"Lord, have mercy on my son" (Matthew 17:15).

"Lord, Son of David, have mercy on me! My daughter is suffering from demon possession" (Matthew 15:22).

"When evening came, many who were demon-possessed were brought to him" (Matthew 8:16).

"When he saw Jesus from a distance, he ran and fell on his knees in front of him" (Mark 5:6).

In each of these instances, someone requested freedom from the demonic: a father asked on behalf of his son, and a mother for her daughter; friends and family asked for those they brought to Jesus; and the demoniac of Gadara, his entire being in torment, instead of fleeing the presence of Jesus ran and fell at His feet.

Principle: Jesus' question, "What do you want me to do for you?" (Matthew 20:32) is always applicable. People in need must not only recognize their need but take the next step of requesting help.

Step 3 - Responsibility

"Who sinned, this man or his parents ...?" (John 9:2).

"Do not let the sun go down while you are still angry, and do not give the devil a foothold" (Ephesians 4:26-27).

"Simon, Simon, Satan has asked to sift you as wheat" (Luke 22:31).

"The Lord said to Satan, 'Very well, then, everything he has is in your hands, but on the man himself do not lay a finger'" (Job 1:12).

After recognizing demonic influence and requesting help, the question of who is responsible arises: Is generational sin and bondage involved? Is the demonic presence due to willful sin by the afflicted person, such as choosing involvement in pornography or the occult? Or, as in the cases of Peter and Job, has God granted Satan limited access to our lives to refine us, making Satan an unwitting tool in God's hand? Peter's three-fold denial of Jesus and Job's loss of everything reveal Satan's activity in their lives, yet both Peter and Job emerged strong men of God.

Principle: Only when responsibility for the affliction is determined can the process of deliverance proceed. In the case of a generational source, detailed knowledge is not necessary for deliverance to take place. In the case of willful sin, the person who chose to sin must now be willing to "own up to it," to accept full responsibility for his/her sinful acts and behavior.

Step 4 - Repentance

"If we claim to be without sin, we deceive ourselves and the truth is not in us. If we confess our sins, he is faithful and just and will forgive us our sins and purify us from all unrighteousness" (1 John 1:8-9).

Confession and repentance go together. In confession, we agree with God about our sins. In repentance, we change the way we think about ourselves, God, our condition, and evil, allowing God to bring our thinking into line with His. Only as we confess and repent is God able to respond to our request for help.

Principle: Confessing the truth and repenting, or changing the way we think about our sin, are basic biblical requirements for God's intervention in our need. To request help, but not confess and repent, results in not receiving the help requested.

Step 5 - Renunciation

"He who conceals his sins does not prosper, but whoever confesses and renounces them finds mercy" (Proverbs 28:13).

"We have renounced secret and shameful ways" (2 Corinthians 4:2).

"This is what the Sovereign Lord says: Repent! Turn from your idols and renounce all your detestable practices!" (Ezekiel 14:6).

Renounce comes from the Latin "renunciare," meaning literally "to tell back," to give back to a messenger the message he has delivered. When we renounce something, we give it up, cast it off, abandon and forsake it.

In the spiritual realm, particularly with involvement in the occult, it means we "tell or give back" what we once chose to receive, that is, the deceit and lies accompanying our sin and occult involvement. A person involved in witchcraft or astrology, for example, might say "I renounce all the lies and darkness in the witchcraft/astrology I once invited and welcomed into my life." It is much like a person's changing citizenship and renouncing all former allegiances.

Principle: Just as we choose to submit ourselves to darkness, so we are able, in Christ, to renounce that authority and turn away from it. This is important especially where the occult is involved. "No one can serve two masters" (Matthew 6:24).

Step 6 - Rebuking

"Jesus rebuked the demon, and it came out of the boy, and he was healed from that moment" (Matthew 17:18).

"But when Jesus turned and looked at his disciples, he rebuked Peter. 'Out of my sight, Satan!' he said" (Mark 8:33).

In the Gospels Jesus rebuked natural elements — wind and waves (Mark 4:39); His disciples for their lack of faith in His resurrection (Mark 16:14); a physical illness (Luke 4:39); and evil spirits (Mark 9:25; Luke 4:41; 9:42). Rebuke, from the Old French meaning "to beat back," involves censuring and declaring authority over a situation, person or entity. In rebuking evil spirits, those praying declare their position and intent, as well as their power over the evil spirit(s).

Principle: Only those who submit to the authority of Jesus have power to rebuke (censure, have power over) an evil spirit. Those who do submit to Jesus' authority should exercise this power when necessary to free a person from demonic bondage.

Step 7 - Releasing

"Whatever you bind on earth will be bound in heaven, and whatever you loose on earth will be loosed in heaven" (Matthew 16:19; 18:18).

"The reason the Son of God appeared was to destroy the devil's work" (1 John 3:8).

The same Greek verb is used in Matthew "whatever you loose" as in 1 John "destroy." The word generally includes the suggestion of destroying, undoing or dissolving that which forms the bond of cohesion. The principle of binding and loosing was taught in the rabbinical schools of Jesus' time. It was based on the investment of authority in a person that enabled him to bind or forbid, and to loose or permit.

When an evil spirit is confronted with, "I bind you in the name of Jesus," the believer who has authority (because he or she is under it) is forbidding the evil spirit to torment any longer.

Similarly, "I command you to loose your hold on _____ in the name of Jesus" expresses the authority to loose or permit the evil spirit to leave. In casting the demons out of the demoniac of Gadara, Jesus exercised this "power to permit" by granting the demons their request to be allowed, in leaving the man, to enter a herd of pigs (Matthew 8:28-34; Mark 5:1-20; Luke 8:26-39).

Principle: Those under authority have authority to bind (forbid) and loose (permit) in relation to the activity of evil spirits in the lives of those who have turned to Jesus and requested His help.

Step 8 - Renewal

"They found the man from whom the demons had gone out, sitting at Jesus' feet, dressed and in his right mind" (Luke 8:35).

"When an evil spirit comes out of a man, it goes through arid places seeking rest and does not find it. Then it says, 'I will return to the house I left.' When it arrives, it finds the house swept clean and put in order. Then it goes and takes seven other spirits more wicked than itself, and they go in and live there. And the final condition of that man is worse than the first" (Luke 11:24-26).

"Therefore, I urge you, brothers, in view of God's mercy, to offer your bodies as living sacrifices, holy and pleasing to God — which is your spiritual worship. Do not conform any longer to the pattern of this world, but be transformed by the renewing of your mind. Then you will be able to test and approve what God's will is — his good, pleasing and perfect will." (Romans 12:1-2).

After Jesus cast the demons out of the man of Gadara, the man's inner self, including his mind, was renewed. Repentance and renewal go together. Both involve changing from a fallen perspective to God's perspective of the way the mind thinks, discerns, evaluates. Removing the demonic influence is only part of deliverance; the other part is putting something in its place — a principle Jesus illustrates in His story of the evil spirit seeking lodging.

Principle: The purpose of deliverance is not the removal of an evil spirit, but the renewal of a life by God. To accomplish the former without seeking the latter is to leave the house "swept clean" but available for the evil spirit's return.

Step 9 - Referral

"Then Jesus said to him, 'See that you don't tell anyone. But go, show yourself to the priest and offer the gift that Moses commanded'" (Matthew 8:4).

"When Jesus saw his mother there, and the disciple whom he loved standing nearby, he said to his mother, 'Dear woman, here is your son,' and to the disciple, 'Here is your mother.' From that time on, this disciple took her into his home" (John 19:26-27).

"I commend to you sister Phoebe, a servant of the church in Cenchrea. I ask you to receive her in the Lord in a way worthy of the saints and to give her any help she may need from you" (Romans 16:1-2).

Jesus referred a healed leper to the appropriate authority of the day for certification of medical and ritual cleanness. He referred His mother and John to one another for their mutual care and growth. Paul referred a member of the church to others asking them to help her with her needs.

Referral is no less needed today. After a demonic presence has left through prayer, it is sometimes appropriate to provide the person with medical care, psychological support through professional counseling, or the ongoing care of a Christian support group or one-on-one support relationship.

Principle: People are best helped in gaining and keeping freedom from the demonic when prayers for deliverance are offered in the context of an extended community providing ongoing support.

Step 10 - Restoration

"As Jesus was getting into the boat, the man who had been demon-possessed begged to go with him. Jesus did not let him, but said, 'Go home to your family and tell them how much the Lord has done for you, and how he has had mercy on you'" (Mark 5:18-19; Luke 8:38-39).

"Brothers, if someone is caught in a sin, you who are spiritual should restore him gently" (Galatians 6:1).

"Restore to me the joy of your salvation" (Psalm 51:12).

The verb Paul used in his admonition to the Galatians means to restore, repair, reinstate. Sometimes the presence of the demonic in a person's life results in strained or broken relationships with others. Jesus sent the demoniac back not so much to talk about deliverance, but to allow the healing he had experienced to touch his family also, people whose lives had been damaged by the frustration and fear of having such a man in their home and having finally to expel him to live in the tombs. Yet they never forgot him, never stopped loving him. Jesus' act of deliverance began a process of restoration in that family. Sometimes, as Paul reminds us, the restoration is of an individual to the body of believers.

As people are set free from demonic powers they have served, they need restoration of what was lost to those powers, what was taken by them. David's prayer following serious sin in the penitential Psalm 51:7-12 is an appropriate prayer for this purpose.

Principle: Restoration, by a person to others who have been wronged, or of an individual life to the lives of others, is often part of the follow-up in the days and weeks after deliverance. God also seeks to restore what the evil one has taken. Those delivered need guidance and assistance in this process.

Step 11 - Relationships

"Many women were there, watching from a distance. They had followed Jesus from Galilee to care for his needs. Among them were Mary Magdalene ..." (Matthew 27:55-56).

"Greet Priscilla and Aquila and the household of Onesiphorus. Erastus stayed in Corinth, and I left Trophimus sick in Miletus ... Eubulus greets you, and so do Pudens, Linus, Claudia and all the brothers" (2 Timothy 4:19-21).

Many women were at the cross including Mary Magdalene "out of whom," Mark 16:9 says, "he had driven seven demons." Paul frequently included lists of names in his letters, indicating relationships that had developed between Christians. A woman freed from the demonic and others who left the darkness of immoral pagan worship found themselves with a new ingredient in their lives: valued relationships, people they loved and who loved them. The reason those who are sick are told to call the elders for prayer is that God knows that prayer works best and has the most lasting effects in the context of relationships. Those being set free from demonic influence will find spiritual protection in committing to a group of Christians and in submitting to that group's spiritual leadership and care.

Principle: God's healing work in our lives is never intended to take place in isolation, but rather in the context of relationships.

Step 12 - Redirection

"When Jesus rose early on the first day of the week, he appeared first to Mary Magadalene, out of whom he had driven seven demons. She went and told those who had been with him and who were mourning and weeping" (Mark 16:9-10).

"Simon, Simon, Satan has asked to sift you as wheat. But I have prayed for you, Simon, that your faith many not fail. And when you have turned back, strengthen your brothers" (Luke 22:31-32).

The process of redirecting a life that at one time has been influenced by the evil one can be seen in the lives of Mary Magdalene and Peter: in Mary after her freedom from demonic bondage; in Peter before Satan successfully tempts him to deny Jesus three times. In both cases healing comes in part through having life turned in a new direction. No empty space is left where the evil one once influenced. Rather, the Lord fills those spaces through redirecting those involved toward the things of God.

Principle: A person freed from a wrong direction needs Christian guidance in the right direction as part of the delivering and healing process.

These twelve steps are guidelines, not hard and fast steps to be followed in strict order. As prayer for deliverance is offered, most, if not all, of these principles will be needed and helpful along the way.

DISCUSSION QUESTIONS:
1. Which of these twelve steps do you find most comfortable for you to consider? Why? What experience have you had with this particular principle or step?
2. Which of these twelve steps is most alien to your thinking? Why?
3. Can you think of other steps which might also help in praying for people tormented in some way by the evil one?

VII
Deliverance: Keeping it in Perspective

How do we keep all of what we have studied in perspective, so the demonic and the evil one are neither ignored nor predominant in our thinking?

Deliverance and Healing

Michael and Dennis Linn, Jesuit psychotherapists, write: "One of the very first principles to be grasped is that deliverance makes sense only in the context of healing. Deliverance, outside the context of healing, runs the risk of becoming a monster. The fact is that there is in truth no such thing as a 'deliverance ministry' — only a healing ministry in which deliverance plays a role. The goal (causa finalis) of healing is wholeness in Christ, an integrated person in relationship to God and others."[20]

This observation is supported by Scripture, where Jesus healed those afflicted by demons (see Scripture charts in appendices). Where deliverance has gotten out of hand it has been due, at least in part, to severing it from the larger context of the healing ministry of the church.

Deliverance and the Helping Professions

The involvement of the larger community of faith, if possible, including physicians, psychiatrists, psychologists and others in helping professions can insure balance and continuity. No ministry functions well with a "lone ranger" approach, least of all this one. The admonition of the wisdom writer in Proverbs 24:6 is valuable when dealing with the demonic. The New International Version reads, "For waging war you need guidance, and for victory many advisors." The King James Version reads, "Where no counsel is, the people fall: but in the multitude of counselors there is safety."

What Next?

Finally, the words of Jesus help to keep this entire matter in perspective. After Jesus sent out the seventy-two, they "returned with joy" Luke 10:17-20 says, "and said, 'Lord, even the demons submit to us in your name.' He replied, 'I saw Satan fall like lightning from heaven. I have given you authority to trample on snakes and scorpions, and to overcome all the power of the enemy; nothing will harm you. However, do not rejoice that the spirits submit to you, but rejoice that your names are written in heaven.'"

DISCUSSION QUESTIONS:
1. What practices or safeguards do you feel can help keep such a ministry in perspective and balance in your local church?
2. What have you learned from this study that is new to you?
3. Where do you plan to go from here in your study of this topic and in applying what you have learned?

Endnotes

1. Karl Barth, *Prayer*, translated by Sara Terrien, Westminster Press, Philadelphia, 1962, p. 76.
2. *The Work of the Holy Spirit*, General Assembly of the United Presbyterian Church, U.S.A., 1970, pp. 20-21.
3. The New England Bible and The Jerusalem Bible.
4. The New International Version and The Berkeley Version.
5. Today's English Version/Good News for Modern Man.
6. The Confession of 1967, 9.09, Presbyterian Church (U.S.A.).
7. *Institutes of the Christian Religion*, John Calvin, I.14.16, Library of Christian Classics, Westminster Press, p. 175.
8. *Theology of the New Testament*, Rudolf Bultmann, Vol. 1, Charles Scribners and Sons, New York, 1951, p. 7.
9. *Spiritual Warfare*, by Michael Harper, Logos International, Plainfield, New Jersey, 1970, Introduction.
10. Voice Magazine, October 1986, p. 30.
11. *Christian Faith and Health*, The United Presbyterian Church in the U.S.A., 1960, p. 14.
12. *Deliverance From Evil Spirits*, Michael Scanlon, T.O.R., and Randall J. Cirner, Servant Books, Ann Arbor, Michigan, 1980.
13. *Evangelical Dictionary of Theology*, Walter Elwell, ed., Baker Book House, Grand Rapids, Michigan, 1984, p. 307.
14. *Power Healing*, by John Wimber with Kevin Springer, Harper and Row, New York, 1987, p. 115.
15. *Demon Possession*, by John L. Nevius, Kregel Publications, Grand Rapids, Michigan, 1968, p. 78.
16. *Demon Possession*, John Warwick Montgomery, ed., Bethany House, Minneapolis, Minnesota, 1976, p. 224.
17. *Deliverance Prayer*, Matthew Linn, S.J., and Dennis Linn, S.J., Paulist Press, New York, New York, 1981, p. 165.
18. *Deliverance From Evil Spirits*, op. cit., pp. 79-80.
19. Ibid, pp. 106-108.
20. *Deliverance Prayer*, op. cit., p. 165.

Appendices

1. THE MINISTRY OF JESUS

Incidents	Matt	Mark	Luke	John
1. Jesus tempted by Satan	4:1-11	1:12-13	4:1-13	
2. Unclean spirit in man in synagogue		1:21-28	4:31-37	
3. Healing demon possessed		1:29-34	4:38-41	
4. Jesus preaching, casting out demons		1:39		
5. Unclean spirits cry out, ordered out		3:10-12		
6. Healing demoniacs	4:23-24		6:17-18	
7. Healing demon possessed	8:14-17	1:29-34	4:38-41	
8. Curing those with evil spirits			7:18-23	
9. Healing of women with evil spirits			8:2	
10. Healing of Gadarene demoniacs	8:28-34	5:1-20	8:26-39	
11. Healing of demonized mute	9:32			
12. Healing of demonized blind/mute man	12:22		11:14	
13. Jesus' power over demons	12:23-30	3:20-30	11:15-23	
14. Unclean spirit seeking lodging	12:43-45		11:24-26	
15. The evil one steals seed sown	13:18	4:15	8:12	
16. The enemy sows weeds among seed	13:25			
17. The weeds and enemy explained	13:38-39			
18. Canaanite girl demon possessed	15:21-28	7:24-30		
19. Peter's words attributed to Satan	16:21-23	8:31-33		
20. Casting out of convulsive spirit	17:14-21	9:14-29	9:37-43	
21. Judgement for the devil, his angels	25:41			
22. Demons cast out of Mary Magdalene		16:9	8:2	
23. Woman healed of spirit of infirmity			13:10-17	
24. Jesus casts out demons, performs cures			13:32	
25. Satan enters Judas to betray Jesus			22:3	13:27
26. Judas has a devil				6:70/ 13:2
27. Satan seeks to influence Peter			22:31-32	
28. Jesus' trial and the power of darkness			22:53	
29. Jesus accused of having a demon				7:20/ 8:48-52/ 10:19-21
30. The devil: liar and murderer				8:44
31. Ruler of this world cast out				12:31-32
32. Ruler of this world and Jesus				14:30/ 16:11
33. Jesus: protect them from the evil one				17:15

2. THE MINISTRY OF THE DISCIPLES AND APOSTLES

Incident: Gospels/Acts	Matt	Mark	Luke	Acts
1. Power given to 12	10:1	3:15	9:1-2	
2. Command to cast out	10:7-8			
3. 12 drive out demons		6:13		
4. Jews cast out demons		9:38-41	9:49-50	
5. Exorcism as sign		16:17-18		
6. 70 have power over demons			10:17-20	
7. Peter discerns Satan's work				5:3
8. Healing of those with spirits				5:16
9. Deliverance brings joy				8:7-8
10. Jesus' deliverance ministry recalled				10:38
11. Paul discerns the devil				13:10
12. Paul casts out divination spirit				16:16-18
13. Paul used to cast out spirits				19:11-12
14. Evil spirits know Paul's power				19:13-16
15. Paul sent to free from Satan				26:18

3. THE MINISTRY OF THE EARLY CHURCH

Reference	Epistle
1. Principalities, powers can't break power of God's love	Romans 8:38-39
2. Satan will someday be crushed under the believer's feet	Romans 16:20
3. Sometimes rebellious Christians are handed over to Satan	1 Cor. 5:1-5
	1 Tim. 1:20
4. Satan can tempt the married who lack sexual self-control	1 Cor. 7:5
5. Behind idols are demonic powers	1 Cor. 10:14-22
6. The Holy Spirit gives the gift of discernment of spirits	1 Cor. 12:10
7. Knowledge of Satan protects the believer from his works	2 Cor. 2:11
8. Satan - "god of this age" - blinds eyes of unbelievers	2 Cor. 4:4
9. Satan seeks to deceive through false prophets, teachings	2 Cor. 4:3-4
	2 Cor. 11:12-15
	1 Tim. 4:1
10. Unbelievers are in bondage to those "not gods"	Galatians 4:8
11. Jesus has decisive power over all authorities, powers	Eph. 1:21, 3:10
12. Unbelievers follow "the ruler of the kingdom of the air"	Eph. 2:1-2
13. Falsehood and anger can give the devil access	Eph. 4:25-27
14. Desires of the flesh can give Satan access	1 Tim. 5:14-15
15. Spiritual warfare requires specific equipping	Eph. 6:10-18
16. Jesus disarmed all evil spiritual powers on the cross	Col. 2:14-15
17. Satan can hinder the work of the follower of Christ	1 Thess. 2:18
18. Satan will seek to unleash his power before the end	2 Thess. 2:1-12
19. The devil seeks to condemn, ensnare or trap believers	1 Tim. 3:6-7
20. Escape from Satan's snare possible through repentance	2 Tim. 2:25-26
21. The devil's power in death has been destroyed	Hebrews 2:14-15

22.	Demons know who Jesus actually is as God	James 2:19
23.	Some kinds of divisive "wisdom" come from the devil	James 3:14-16
24.	Obedient believers may successfully resist the devil	James 4:7
25.	The devil, our adversary, continually seeks to get us	1 Peter 5:8
26.	In Christ believers have "overcome" the evil one	1 John 2:13-14
27.	Jesus came to destroy the works of the devil	1 John 3:8
28.	People are either children of God or the devil	1 John 3:10
29.	The "spirit of antichrist" is a demonic spirit	1 John 4:1-6
30.	Denying that Jesus is God come in the flesh	2 John 7
31.	All unbelievers in the world are in the evil one's power	1 John 5:19

Bibliography

This is a partial listing of materials available on the subjects of Satan, evil spirits or demons, and deliverance. Care should be taken to avoid materials that attribute all ills and problems to Satan, as well as those publications dealing with evil from an occult perspective. As in all reading, discernment and critical thinking should be exercised.

Banks, William, *Songs of Deliverance*, Impact Books, Kirkwood, Missouri, 1987.

Barnhouse, Donald Grey, *The Invisible War: The Panorama of the Continuing Conflict Between Good and Evil*, Zondervan Publishing House, Grand Rapids, Michigan, 1965.

Basham, Donald, *Can a Christian Have a Demon?* Whitaker Books, Monroeville, Pennsylvania, 1971.

Deliver Us From Evil, Chosen Books, Washington Depot, Connecticut, 1972.

Christian Faith and Health, Office of the General Assembly, United Presbyterian Church, New York, New York, 1960.

Dearing, Trevor, *Supernatural Powers*, Logos International, Plainfield, New Jersey, 1977.

Green, Michael, *I Believe in Satan's Downfall*, William B. Eerdmans Publishing Company, Grand Rapids, Michigan, 1981.

Harper, Michael, *Spiritual Warfare*, Logos International, Plainfield, New Jersey, 1970.

Kallas, James, *Jesus and the Power of Satan*, The Westminster Press, Philadelphia, Pennsylvania, 1968.

The Satanward View: A Study in Pauline Theology, The Westminster Press, Philadelphia, Pennsylvania, 1966.

Koch, Kurt, *Between Christ and Satan*, Kregel Publications, Grand Rapids, Michigan, 1968.

Christian Counseling and Occultism, Kregel Publications, Grand Rapids, Michigan, 1965.

Demonology, Past and Present, Kregel Publications, Grand Rapids, Michigan, 1973.

Devil's Alphabet, The, Kregel Publications, Grand Rapids, Michigan.

Linn, Dennis, S. J., and Linn, Matthew, S. J., *Deliverance Prayer: Experiential, Psychological and Theological Approaches*, Paulist Press, New York, New York, 1981.

McNutt, Francis, O. P., *Healing*, Ave Maria Press, Notre Dame, Indiana, 1974.
The Power of Healing, Ave Maria Press, Notre Dame, Indiana, 1977.
Nevius, John L., *Demon Possession*, Kregel Publications, Grand Rapids, Michigan, 1968.
Peck, M. Scott, M.D., *People of the Lie: The Hope for Healing Human Evil*, Simon and Schuster, New York, New York, 1983.
Pentecost, J. Dwight, *Your Adversary the Devil*, Zondervan Publishing House, Grand Rapids, Michigan, 1969.
Pursey, Barbara, *The Gifts of the Holy Spirit*, Presbyterian Renewal Publications, Oklahoma City, Oklahoma, 1984.
Richards, John, *But Deliver Us From Evil: An Introduction to The Demonic in Pastoral Care*, The Seabury Press, New York, New York 1974.
Scanlon, Michael, T.O.R., and Cirner, Randall, *Deliverance From Evil Spirits: A Weapon For Spiritual Warfare*, Servant Books, Ann Arbor, Michigan, 1980.
Southard, Samuel, *Demonology and Mental Illness: A Problem in Spiritual and Psychological Discernment for Pastor and People*, Fuller Theological Seminary, Pasadena, California, 1985.
Unger, Merrill F., *Biblical Demonology*, Scripture Press Foundation, Wheaton, Illinois, sixth edition, 1965.
Wimber, John, *Power Healing*, Harper and Row Publishers, New York, New York, 1987.
Work of the Holy Spirit, The, General Assembly of the United Presbyterian Church, New York, New York, 1970.

Additional Resources

The tape ministry of the Presbyterian & Reformed Renewal Ministries Int'l. has available teaching tapes on various aspects of the Christian deliverance ministry by Meryl Allinder, Robert Bayley, Brick Bradford, Mike Flynn, Melicent Huneycutt-Vergeer, Lance Pitluck, Barbara Pursey, Don Rogers, William van Dam and others. Write or call: PRRM, 2245 N.W. 39th St., Oklahoma City, OK 73112. 405-525-2552.